CHRISTMAS CAROLS

CHRISTMAS CAROLS

This edition first published in 1985
by Octopus Books Limited
59 Grosvenor Street
London W1

Musical arrangements © Oxford University Press 1985
Design, illustration and introductory text
© Hennerwood Publications Limited 1985

ISBN 0 86273 269 7

Printed by A.G. V. Vicenza, Italy

The carol arrangements are mostly derived from *Carols for Piano* arranged by
Gillian Earl and from *The Oxford Book of Carols,* both published by
Oxford University Press. The words of 'Little Jesus, Sweetly Sleep', and the
words and melody line of 'On Christmas Night' are reprinted from *The Oxford
Book of Carols* by permission of Oxford University Press. The melody of
Forest Green ('O Little Town') was collected and arranged by R. Vaughan Williams
and is reprinted from the *English Hymnal* by permission of Oxford
University Press.

Contents

Introduction

Singing carols is a part of Christmas which can be enjoyed in gatherings both large and small. For some, the mention of carols will bring to mind an outing to church to share in the now traditional service of Nine Lessons and Carols, perhaps by candlelight; for others it will conjure up a picture of a family gathering around the piano, or perhaps the electronic keyboard or synthesiser (possibly newly acquired from Father Christmas). Whatever form such music making takes, it continues a tradition which is centuries old, although many of the 'traditional' carols are the result of much more recent revival and rearrangement.

The word *carol* originally comes from the French *caroler* meaning to dance in a ring. The earliest carols told the biblical stories surrounding the birth of Christ (from the appearance of the Angel Gabriel to the Virgin Mary, through the visits of shepherds and kings to the crib, to Herod's massacre of the Holy Innocents), and they were sung to simple, popular tunes, often with a refrain or chorus repeated after each verse. They were performed when revellers gathered together outside the Church after the festive service to sing and dance in the churchyard. However, such behaviour was generally viewed with considerable disapproval by Mediaeval Church authorities: it was not until the fifteenth century that the popular carol was able to flourish in peaceful coexistence with traditional plainsong chants and other kinds of church music. By this time, carols were admitted inside the church, where they served to provide music for the various Christmas processions (a practice continued in today's Nine Lessons service with the processional entry of the choir during the singing of *Once in Royal David's City*). Once established, the popular folk tradition thrived until it came up against puritanical restraints once more, this time in the form of Cromwell and the Long Parliament, who, apart from throwing up their hands in horror at the mention of dancing, in 1647 abolished the festival of Christmas altogether! Although the Restoration of King Charles II

swiftly brought about the reinstatement of music, dance and drama as courtly entertainment, the folk tradition of carol singing was not so fortunate. It was not until the early years of this century that this rich tradition was rediscovered and performed either in authentic style, or with carols skilfully arranged in keeping with more modern choral style. Meanwhile, in the 1850s one Rev. J. M. Neale discovered a 16th century Swedish carol collection *Piae Cantiones*, and published many items from it in translation (including *Good King Wenceslas*). Thus many of our most popular carols come not from the original folk tradition but from more recent developments — and many more are not originally English. Apart from those found in *Piae Cantiones*, the tune of *Hark the Herald Angels Sing* was written by Mendelssohn and *Silent Night*, as *Stille Nacht*, is still one of Germany's most popular Christmas melodies. Of those which do date back to earlier times, several, like *In Dulci Jubilo* mix Latin and English words — a time-honoured device for popularising and explaining the traditional Latin texts of the Mediaeval Church.

A word about performing the carols in this volume: the accompaniments are very simple, designed to be playable by anyone with a basic knowledge of a keyboard (in other words, Grade I or II standard). But their performance is not restricted to a traditional piano: chord symbols have been added for accompaniment on the guitar (these easy chords are not always the same harmonies as the keyboard accompaniment), while the keyboard parts will also fit happily on to an electronic keyboard. If you use the latter, do experiment with the sounds you create — and remember that, according to legend, the shepherds played on their pipes (try flute or soft reed stops to achieve the effect), while the angels appearing in the heavens proclaimed their message with 'trumpets and timbals, harp and cymbals' (timbals = drums). Suit the style to the mood of the carol, for while many carols encourage us to make merry and to make a merry noise, others are lullabies, originally designed to send an infant to sleep.

Merry Christmas!

Once in Royal David's City

1 Once in royal David's city
Stood a lowly cattle shed,
Where a mother laid her baby
In a manger for his bed:
Mary was that mother mild,
Jesus Christ her little child.

2 He came down to earth from heaven
Who is God and Lord of all,
And his shelter was a stable,
And his cradle was a stall;
With the poor and mean and lowly
Lived on earth our Saviour holy.

3 And our eyes at last shall see him,
Through his own redeeming love,
For that child so dear and gentle
Is our Lord in heaven above;
And he leads his children on
To the place where he is gone.

4 Not in that poor lowly stable,
With the oxen standing by,
We shall see him; but in heaven,
Set at God's right hand on high;
Where like stars his children crowned
All in white shall wait around.

Mrs C. F. Alexander

Once in Royal David's City

H. J. Gauntlett

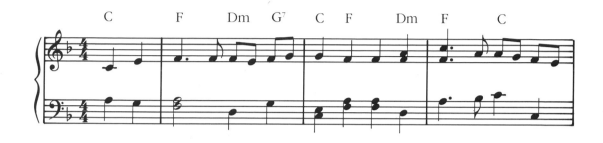

Hark! the Herald Angels Sing

1 Hark! the herald angels sing
Glory to the new-born King;
Peace on earth and mercy mild,
God and sinners reconciled:
Joyful all ye nations rise,
Join the triumph of the skies,
With the angelic host proclaim,
Christ is born in Bethlehem.

Hark! the herald angels sing
Glory to the new-born King.

2 Christ, by highest heav'n adored,
Christ, the everlasting Lord,
Late in time behold him come
Offspring of a virgin's womb:
Veiled in flesh the Godhead see,
Hail the incarnate Deity!
Pleased as man with man to dwell,
Jesus, our Emmanuel.

3 Hail the heaven-born Prince of peace!
Hail the Sun of Righteousness!
Light and life to all he brings,
Risen with healing in his wings;
Mild he lays his glory by,
Born that man no more may die,
Born to raise the sons of earth,
Born to give them second birth.

C. Wesley, T. Whitefield,
M. Madan, and others

Hark! the Herald Angels Sing

Mendelssohn

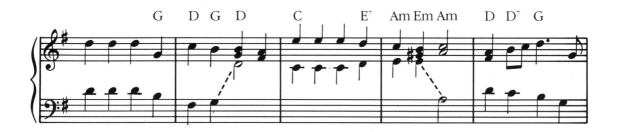

Silent Night

Franz Grüber

1 Silent night, holy night,
  All is dark, save the light
  Shining where the mother mild
  Watches over the holy child.
  Sleep in heavenly peace,
  Sleep in heavenly peace.

2 Silent night, holy night,
  Shepherds first saw the sight,
  Heard the angel-song alleluia,
  Loud proclaiming near and far:
  'Christ our Saviour is here,
  Christ our Saviour is here.'

3 Silent night, holy night,
  God's own son, Oh how bright
  Shines the love in thy holy face,
  Shines the light of redemption and grace,
  Christ th'incarnate God,
  Christ th'incarnate God.

Joseph Mohr,
Tr. David Willcocks

God Rest You Merry, Gentlemen

1 God rest you merry, gentlemen,
Let nothing you dismay,
For Jesus Christ our Saviour
Was born upon this day,
To save us all from Satan's power
When we were gone astray:

O tidings of comfort and joy,
Comfort and joy,
O tidings of comfort and joy.

2 In Bethlehem in Jewry
This blessed babe was born,
And laid within a manger,
Upon this blessed morn;
The which his mother Mary
Nothing did take in scorn:

3 From God our heavenly Father
A blessed angel came,
And unto certain shepherds
Brought tidings of the same,
How that in Bethlehem was born
The Son of God by name:

4 'Fear not,' then said the Angel,
'Let nothing you affright,
This day is born a Saviour,
Of virtue, power, and might;
So frequently to vanquish all
The friends of Satan quite':

5 The shepherds at those tidings
Rejoiced much in mind,
And left their flocks a-feeding,
In tempest, storm, and wind,
And went to Bethlehem straightway
This blessed Babe to find:

6 And when they came to Bethlehem,
Where our sweet Saviour lay,
They found him in a manger,
Where oxen feed on hay;
His mother Mary kneeling,
Unto the Lord did pray:

7 Now to the Lord sing praises
All you within this place,
And with true love and brotherhood
Each other now embrace;
This holy tide of Christmas
All others doth deface:

Traditional

God Rest You Merry, Gentlemen

English traditional carol

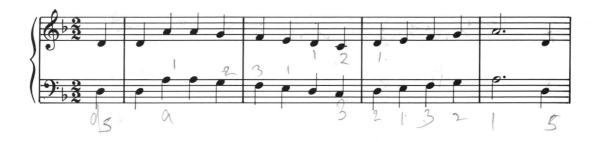

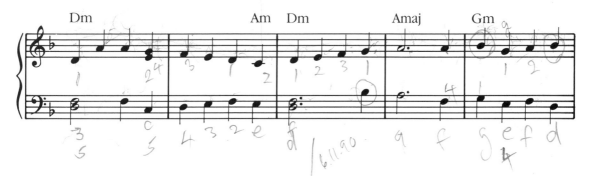

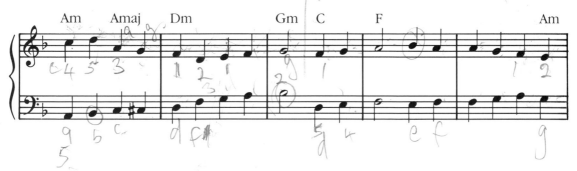

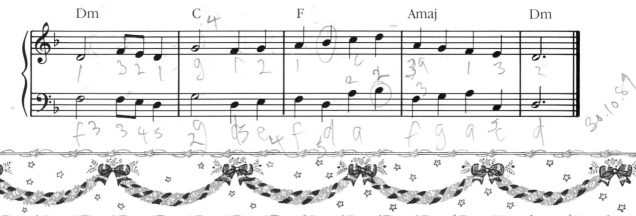

O Little Town of Bethlehem

1 O little town of Bethlehem,
   How still we see thee lie!
   Above thy deep and dreamless sleep
   The silent stars go by.
   Yet in thy dark streets shineth
   The everlasting light;
   The hopes and fears of all the years
   Are met in thee to-night.

2 How silently, how silently,
   The wondrous gift is given!
   So God imparts to human hearts
   The blessings of his heaven.
   No ear may hear his coming;
   But in this world of sin,
   Where meek souls will receive him, still
   The dear Christ enters in.

3 O holy Child of Bethlehem,
   Descend to us, we pray;
   Cast out our sin, and enter in:
   Be born in us today.
   We hear the Christmas angels
   The great glad tidings tell:
   O come to us, abide with us,
   Our Lord Emmanuel.

Bishop Phillips Brooks

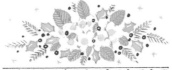

O little Town of Bethlehem

English traditional tune
Collected and adapted by
Ralph Vaughan Williams

See Amid the Winter's Snow

1 See amid the winter's snow,
  Born for us on earth below;
  See the tender Lamb appears,
  Promised from eternal years:

  Hail, thou ever-blessèd morn;
  Hail, redemption's happy dawn;
  Sing through all Jerusalem,
  Christ is born in Bethlehem.

2 Say, ye holy shepherds, say
  What your joyful news to-day;
  Wherefore have ye left your sheep
  On the lonely mountain steep?

3 'As we watched at dead of night,
  Lo, we saw a wondrous light;
  Angels singing "Peace on earth"
  Told us of the Saviour's birth:'

4 Teach, O teach us, Holy Child,
  By thy face so meek and mild,
  Teach us to resemble thee,
  In thy sweet humility:

E. Caswall

See Amid the Winter's Snow

John Goss

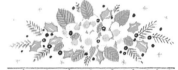

The Infant King

1 Sing lullaby!
   Lullaby baby, now reclining,
   Sing lullaby!
   Hush, do not wake the Infant King.
   Angels are watching, stars are shining
   Over the place where he is lying:
   Sing lullaby!

2 Sing lullaby!
   Lullaby baby, now a-sleeping,
   Sing lullaby!
   Hush, do not wake the Infant King.
   Soon will come sorrow with the morning,
   Soon will come bitter grief and weeping:
   Sing lullaby!

3 Sing lullaby!
   Lullaby baby, now a-dozing,
   Sing lullaby!
   Hush, do not wake the Infant King.
   Soon comes the cross, the nails, the piercing,
   Then in the grave at last reposing:
   Sing lullaby!

4 Sing lullaby!
   Lullaby! is the babe a-waking?
   Sing lullaby!
   Hush, do not stir the Infant King.
   Dreaming of Easter, gladsome morning,
   Conquering Death, its bondage breaking:
   Sing lullaby!

S. Baring-Gould

The Infant King

Basque carol

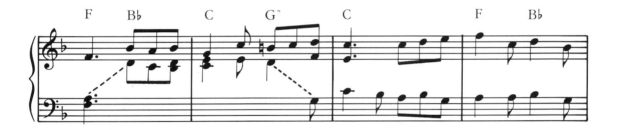

The First Nowell

1 The first Nowell the angel did say
Was to certain poor shepherds in fields as they lay;
In fields where they lay, keeping their sheep,
On a cold winter's night that was so deep:

Nowell, Nowell, Nowell, Nowell,
Born is the King of Israel.

2 They lookèd up and saw a star,
Shining in the east, beyond them far;
And to the earth it gave great light,
And so it continued both day and night:

3 And by the light of that same star,
Three Wise Men came from country far;
To seek for a king was their intent,
And to follow the star wherever it went:

4 This star drew nigh to the north-west;
O'er Bethlehem it took its rest,
And there it did both stop and stay
Right over the place where Jesus lay:

5 Then entered in those Wise Men three,
Full reverently upon their knee,
And offered there in his presence
Their gold and myrrh and frankincense:

6 Then let us all with one accord
Sing praises to our heav'nly Lord,
That hath made heav'n and earth of naught,
And with his blood mankind hath bought:

The First Nowell

Traditional English carol

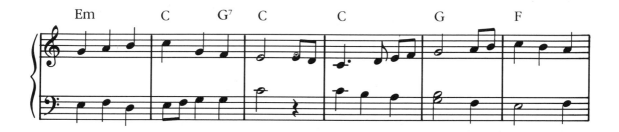

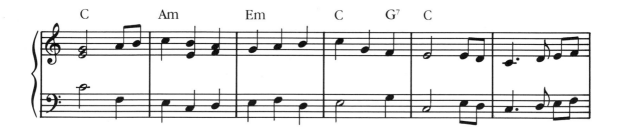

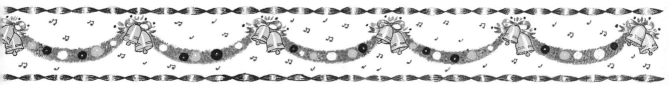

Away in a Manger

1 Away in a manger, no crib for a bed,
   The little Lord Jesus laid down his sweet head.
   The stars in the bright sky looked down where he lay,
   The little Lord Jesus asleep in the hay.

2 The cattle are lowing, the baby awakes,
   But little Lord Jesus no crying he makes.
   I love thee, Lord Jesus! Look down from the sky,
   And stay by my side until morning is nigh.

3 Be near me, Lord Jesus; I ask thee to stay
   Close by me for ever, and love me, I pray.
   Bless all the dear children in thy tender care,
   And fit us for heaven, to live with thee there.

Anon.

Away in a Manger

W. J. Kirkpatrick

While Shepherds Watched

1 While shepherds watched their flocks by night,
All seated on the ground,
The angel of the Lord came down,
And glory shone around.

2 'Fear not', said he (for mighty dread
Had seized their troubled mind);
'Glad tidings of great joy I bring
To you and all mankind.

3 'To you in David's town this day
Is born of David's line
A Saviour, who is Christ the Lord;
And this shall be the sign:

4 'The heavenly Babe you there shall find
To human view displayed,
All meanly wrapped in swathing bands,
And in a manger laid.'

5 Thus spake the seraph; and forthwith
Appeared a shining throng
Of angels praising God, who thus
Addressed their joyful song:

6 'All glory be to God on high,
And to the earth be peace;
Good-will henceforth from heaven to men
Begin and never cease.'

Nahum Tate

While Shepherds Watched

Este's Psalter, 1592

Mid-Winter

1 In the bleak mid-winter
   Frosty wind made moan,
   Earth stood hard as iron
   Water like a stone;
   Snow had fallen, snow on snow,
   Snow on snow,
   In the bleak mid-winter,
   Long ago.

2 Our God, heav'n cannot hold him
   Nor earth sustain;
   Heav'n and earth shall flee away
   When he comes to reign:
   In the bleak mid-winter
   A stable-place sufficed
   The Lord God Almighty
   Jesus Christ.

3 Enough for him, whom cherubim
   Worship night and day,
   A breastful of milk,
   And a mangerful of hay;
   Enough for him, whom angels
   Fall down before,
   The ox and ass and camel
   Which adore.

4 What can I give him
   Poor as I am?
   If I were a shepherd
   I would bring a lamb;
   If I were a wise man
   I would do my part;
   Yet what I can I give him—
   Give my heart.

Christina Rossetti

Mid-Winter

G. Holst

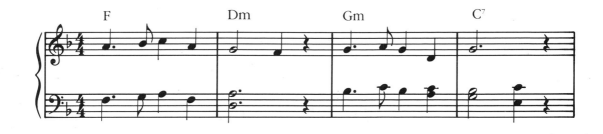

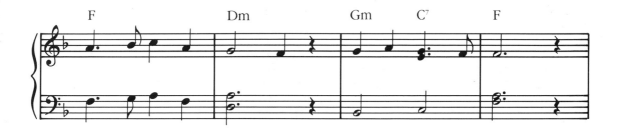

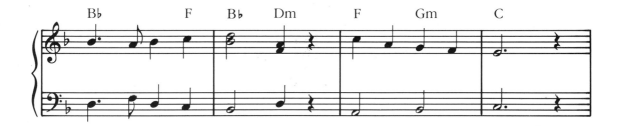

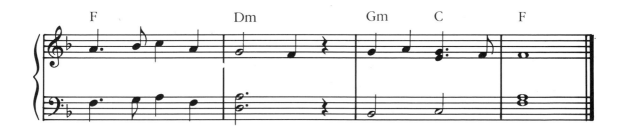

Good King Wenceslas

1 Good King Wenceslas looked out,
On the Feast of Stephen,
When the snow lay round about,
Deep, and crisp, and even:
Brightly shone the moon that night,
Though the frost was cruel,
When a poor man came in sight,
Gathering winter fuel.

2 'Hither, page, and stand by me,
If thou know'st it, telling,
Yonder peasant, who is he?
Where and what his dwelling?'
'Sire, he lives a good league hence,
Underneath the mountain,
Right against the forest fence,
By St. Agnes' fountain.'

3 'Bring me flesh, and bring me wine,
Bring me pine-logs hither:
Thou and I will see him dine,
When we bear them thither.'
Page and monarch, forth they went,
Forth they went together;
Through the rude wind's wild lament
And the bitter weather.

4 'Sire, the night is darker now,
And the wind blows stronger;
Fails my heart, I know not how;
I can go no longer.'
'Mark my footsteps, good my page;
Tread thou in them boldly:
Thou shalt find the winter's rage
Freeze thy blood less coldly.'

5 In his master's steps he trod,
Where the snow lay dinted;
Heat was in the very sod
Which the Saint had printed.
Therefore, Christian men, be sure,
Wealth or rank possessing,
Ye who now will bless the poor,
Shall yourselves find blessing.

J. M. Neale

Good King Wenceslas

Tune from *Piae Cantiones,* 1582

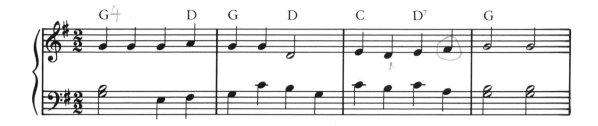

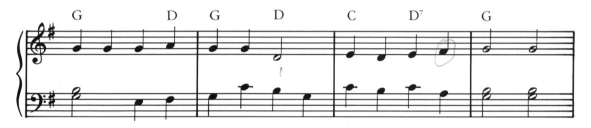

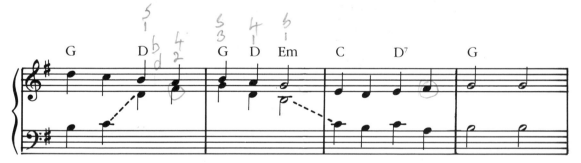

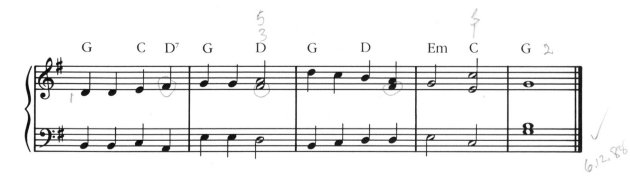

The Holly and the Ivy

1 The holly and the ivy,
   When they are both full grown,
   Of all the trees that are in the wood
   The holly bears the crown:

   The rising of the sun
   And the running of the deer,
   The playing of the merry organ,
   Sweet singing in the choir.

2 The holly bears a blossom,
   As white as any flower,
   And Mary bore sweet Jesus Christ
   To be our sweet Saviour:

3 The holly bears a berry,
   As red as any blood,
   And Mary bore sweet Jesus Christ
   To do poor sinners good:

4 The holly bears a prickle,
   As sharp as any thorn,
   And Mary bore sweet Jesus Christ
   On Christmas day in the morn:

5 The holly and the ivy,
   When they are both full grown,
   Of all the trees that are in the wood
   The holly bears the crown:

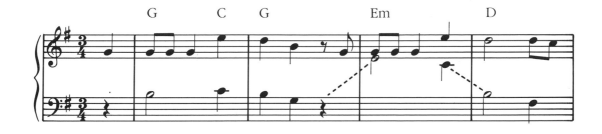

The Holly and the Ivy

English traditional carol

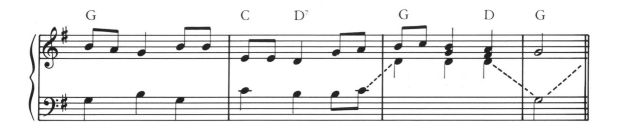

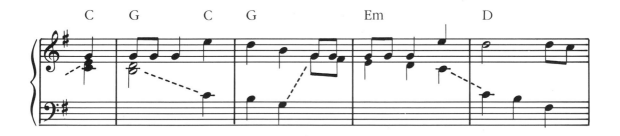

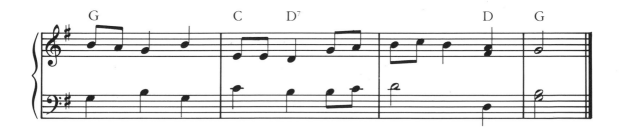

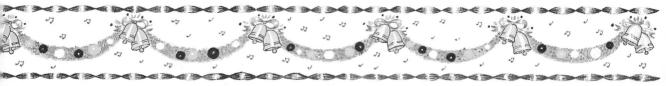

O Come, All Ye Faithful

1 O come, all ye faithful,
   Joyful and triumphant,
   O come ye, O come ye to Bethlehem;
   Come and behold him
   Born the King of Angels:

   O come, let us adore him,
   O come, let us adore him,
   O come, let us adore him, Christ the Lord!

2 God of God,
   Light of light,
   Lo! he abhors not the Virgin's womb;
   Very God,
   Begotten not created:

3 Sing, choirs of angels,
   Sing in exultation,
   Sing, all ye citizens of heav'n above;
   Glory to God
   In the highest:

4 Yea, Lord, we greet thee,
   Born this happy morning,
   Jesu, to thee be glory giv'n;
   Word of the Father,
   Now in flesh appearing:

                    Tr. F. Oakeley,
            W. T. Brooke and others

O Come, All Ye Faithful

Composer unknown
(probably 18th century)

As With Gladness

C. Kocher

1 As with gladness men of old
  Did the guiding star behold,
  As with joy they hailed its light,
  Leading onward, beaming bright,
  So, most gracious God, may we
  Evermore be led to thee.

2 As with joyful steps they sped,
  To that lowly manger-bed,
  There to bend the knee before
  Him whom heaven and earth adore,
  So may we with willing feet
  Ever seek thy mercy-seat.

3 As they offered gifts most rare
  At that manger rude and bare,
  So may we with holy joy,
  Pure, and free from sin's alloy,
  All our costliest treasures bring,
  Christ, to thee our heavenly King.

4 Holy Jesu, every day
  Keep us in the narrow way;
  And, when earthly things are past,
  Bring our ransomed souls at last
  Where they need no star to guide,
  Where no clouds thy glory hide.

W. C. Dix

Angels, From the Realms of Glory

1 Angels, from the realms of glory,
Wing your flight through all the earth;
Ye who sang creation's story
Now proclaim Messiah's birth:

Come and worship
Christ the new-born King,
Come and worship,
Worship Christ the new-born King.

2 Shepherds in the field abiding,
Watching o'er your flocks by night,
God with man is now residing;
Yonder shines the infant light:

3 Sages, leave your contemplations;
Brighter visions beam afar;
See the great Desire of Nations;
Ye have seen his natal star:

4 Saints before the altar bending,
Watching long in hope and fear,
Suddenly the Lord, descending,
In his temple shall appear:

5 Though an infant now we view him,
He shall fill his Father's throne,
Gather all the nations to him;
Every knee shall then bow down:

James Montgomery

Angels, From the Realms of Glory

Old French Tune

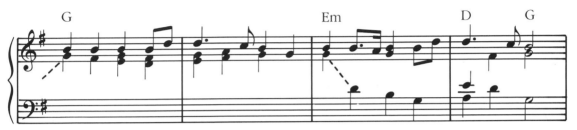

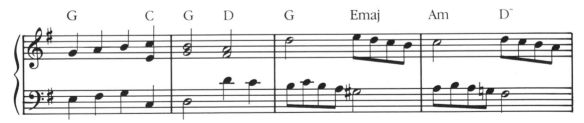

Ding Dong! Merrily on High

1 Ding dong! merrily on high
In heaven the bells are ringing:
Ding dong! verily the sky
Is riven with angels singing:
Gloria, Hosanna in excelsis!

2 E'en so here below, below,
Let steeple bells be swungen,
And *i-o, i-o, i-o,*
By priest and people sungen:
Gloria, Hosanna in excelsis!

3 Pray you, dutifully prime
Your matin chime, ye ringers;
May you beautifully rime
Your eve-time song, ye singers:
Gloria, Hosanna in excelsis!

Tr. G. R. Woodward

Ding Dong! Merrily on High

16th-century French tune

Coventry Carol

Lully, lulla, thou little tiny child,
By, by, lully lullay.

1 O sisters too,
How may we do
For to preserve this day
This poor youngling,
For whom we do sing,
By by, lully lullay?

2 Herod, the king,
In his raging,
Chargèd he hath this day
His men of might,
In his own sight,
All young children to slay.

3 That woe is me,
Poor child for thee!
And ever morn and day,
For thy parting
Neither say nor sing
By by, lully lullay!

from Pageant of the Shearmen and
Tailors, Fifteenth Century

Coventry Carol

Tune of 1591

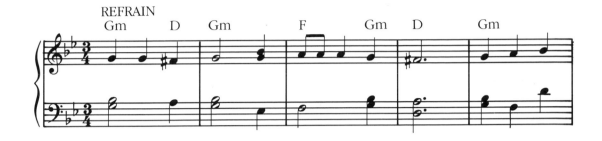

Repeat Refrain after verse 3

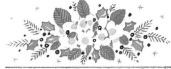

Little Jesus, Sweetly Sleep

Czech carol

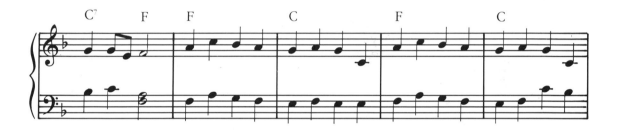

1 Little Jesus, sweetly sleep, do not stir;
  We will lend a coat of fur,
  We will rock you, rock you, rock you,
  We will rock you, rock you, rock you:
  See the fur to keep you warm,
  Snugly round your tiny form.

2 Mary's little baby, sleep, sweetly sleep,
  Sleep in comfort, slumber deep;
  We will rock you, rock you, rock you,
  We will rock you, rock you, rock you:
  We will serve you all we can,
  Darling, darling little man.

Tr. P. Dearmer

In Dulci Jubilo

1 In dulci jubilo
   Let us our homage show;
   Our heart's joy reclineth
   In praesepio
   And like a bright star shineth,
   Matris in gremio.
   Alpha es et O,
   Alpha es et O.

2 O Jesu parvule!
   My heart is sore for thee!
   Hear me, I beseech thee,
   O Puer optime!
   My prayer let it reach thee,
   O Princeps gloriae!
   Trahe me post te!
   Trahe me post te!

3 O Patris caritas,
   O Nati lenitas!
   Deeply were we stainèd
   Per nostra crimina;
   But thou for us hast gainèd
   Coelorum gaudia.
   O that we were there!
   O that we were there!

4 Ubi sunt gaudia,
   If that they be not there?
   There are angels singing
   Nova cantica,
   There the bells are ringing
   In Regis curia:
   O that we were there!
   O that we were there!

Tr. R. L. Pearsall

In Dulci Jubilo

Old German carol

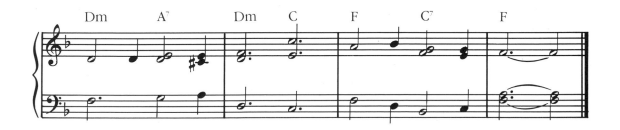

Infant Holy

1 Infant holy, infant lowly,
   For his bed a cattle stall;
   Oxen lowing, little knowing
   Christ the Babe is Lord of all.
   Swift are winging angels singing,
   Nowells ringing, tidings bringing,
   Christ the Babe is Lord of all,
   Christ the Babe is Lord of all.

2 Flocks were sleeping, shepherds keeping
   Vigil till the morning new;
   Saw the glory, heard the story,
   Tidings of a gospel true.
   Thus rejoicing, free from sorrow,
   Praises voicing, greet the morrow,
   Christ the Babe was born for you!
   Christ the Babe was born for you!

Infant Holy

Tr. Edith M. Reed

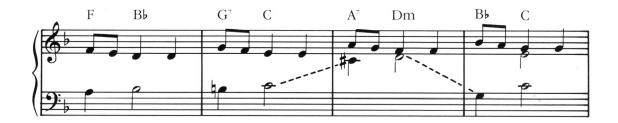

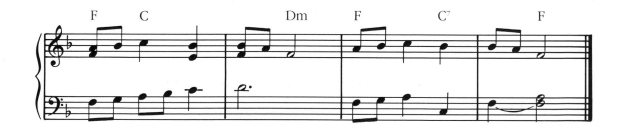

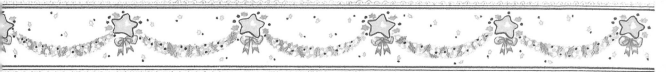

It Came Upon the Midnight Clear

1 It came upon the midnight clear,
That glorious song of old,
From angels bending near the earth
To touch their harps of gold:
'Peace on the earth, good-will to men,
From heav'n's all-gracious King!'
The world in solemn stillness lay
To hear the angels sing.

2 Still through the cloven skies they come,
With peaceful wings unfurled;
And still their heav'nly music floats
O'er all the weary world;
Above its sad and lowly plains
They bend on hov'ring wing;
And ever o'er its Babel sounds
The blessed angels sing.

3 Yet with the woes of sin and strife
The world has suffered long;
Beneath the angel-strain have rolled
Two thousand years of wrong;
And man, at war with man, hears not
The love-song which they bring:
O hush the noise ye men of strife,
And hear the angels sing!

4 For lo! the days are hastening on,
By prophet-bards foretold,
When, with the ever-circling years,
Comes round the age of gold;
When peace shall over all the earth
Its ancient splendours fling,
And the whole world send back the song
Which now the angels sing.

E. H. Seers

It Came Upon the Midnight Clear

Traditional English tune
adapted by Arthur Sullivan

I Saw Three Ships

English traditional carol

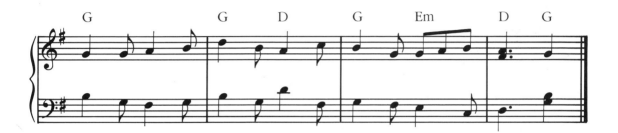

1 I saw three ships come sailing in,
   On Christmas Day, on Christmas Day,
   I saw three ships come sailing in,
   On Christmas Day in the morning.

2 And what was in those ships all three?

3 Our Saviour Christ and his lady.

4 Pray, whither sailed those ships all three?

5 O, they sailed into Bethlehem.

6 And all the bells on earth shall ring.

7 And all the angels in heaven shall sing.

8 And all the souls on earth shall sing.

9 Then let us all rejoice amain!

Traditional

Sussex Carol

1 On Christmas night all Christians sing,
 To hear the news the angels bring,
 On Christmas night all Christians sing,
 To hear the news the angels bring—
 News of great joy, news of great mirth,
 News of our merciful King's birth.

2 Then why should men on earth be so sad,
 Since our Redeemer made us glad,
 Then why should men on earth be so sad,
 Since our Redeemer made us glad,
 When from our sin he set us free,
 All for to gain our liberty?

3 When sin departs before his grace,
 Then life and health come in its place;
 When sin departs before his grace,
 Then life and health come in its place:
 Angels and men with joy may sing,
 All for to see the new-born King.

4 All out of darkness we have light,
 Which made the angels sing this night,
 All out of darkness we have light,
 Which made the angels sing this night:
 'Glory to God and peace to men,
 Now and for evermore. Amen.'

Sussex Carol

Traditional

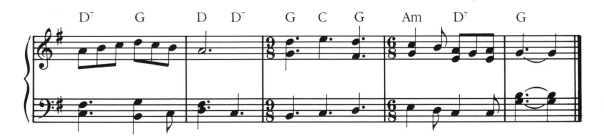

The Angel Gabriel

1 The angel Gabriel from heaven came,
His wings as drifted snow, his eyes as flame;
'All hail,' said he, 'thou lowly maiden Mary,
Most highly favour'd lady,'
Gloria!

2 'For known a blessèd Mother thou shalt be,
All generations laud and honour thee,
Thy son shall be Emmanuel, by seers foretold.
Most highly favour'd lady,'
Gloria!

3 Then gentle Mary meekly bowed her head,
'To me be as it pleaseth God,' she said,
'My soul shall laud and magnify His Holy Name.'
Most highly favour'd lady,
Gloria!

4 Of her, Emmanuel, the Christ, was born
In Bethlehem, all on a Christmas morn,
And Christian folk throughout the world will ever say—
Most highly favour'd lady,
Gloria!

S. Baring-Gould

The Angel Gabriel

Basque carol

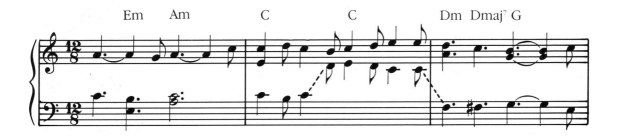

Unto Us is Born a Son

Tune from *Piae Cantiones,* 1582

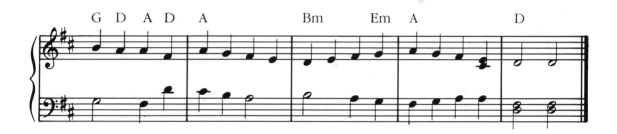

1 Unto us is born a Son,
  King of quires supernal:
  See on earth his life begun,
  Of lords the Lord eternal,
  Of lords the Lord eternal.

2 Christ, from heav'n descending low,
  Comes on earth a stranger;
  Ox and ass their owner know,
  Becradled in the manger,
  Becradled in the manger.

3 This did Herod sore affray,
  And grievously bewilder,
  So he gave the word to slay,
  And slew the little childer,
  And slew the little childer.

4 Of his love and mercy mild
  This the Christmas story;
  And O that Mary's gentle child
  Might lead us up to glory,
  Might lead us up to glory!

5 O and A, and A and O,
  Cum cantibus in choro,
  Let our merry organ go,
  Benedicamus Domino,
  Benedicamus Domino.

Tr. G. R. Woodward

We Three Kings

1 We three kings of Orient are;
   Bearing gifts we traverse afar
   Field and fountain, moor and mountain,
   Following yonder star:

   O star of wonder, star of night,
   Star with royal beauty bright,
   Westward leading, still proceeding,
   Guide us to thy perfect light.

2 Born a king on Bethlehem plain,
   Gold I bring, to crown him again—
   King for ever, ceasing never,
   Over us all to reign:

3 Frankincense to offer have I;
   Incense owns a Deity nigh:
   Prayer and praising, all men raising,
   Worship him, God most high:

4 Myrrh is mine; its bitter perfume
   Breathes a life of gathering gloom;
   Sorrowing, sighing, bleeding, dying,
   Sealed in the stone-cold tomb:

5 Glorious now, behold him arise,
   King, and God, and sacrifice!
   Alleluia, alleluia;
   Earth to the heavens replies:

J. H. Hopkins

We Three Kings

J. H. Hopkins

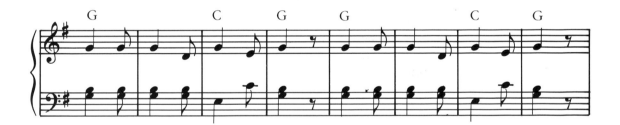

We Wish You a Merry Christmas

1 We wish you a merry Christmas,
 We wish you a merry Christmas,
 We wish you a merry Christmas,
 And a happy New Year.

 Good tidings we bring to you and your kin;
 We wish you a merry Christmas
 And a happy New Year.

2 Now bring us some figgy pudding,
 Now bring us some figgy pudding,
 Now bring us some figgy pudding,
 And bring some out here.

3 For we all like figgy pudding,
 For we all like figgy pudding,
 For we all like figgy pudding,
 So bring some out here.

4 And we won't go until we've got some,
 And we won't go until we've got some,
 And we won't go until we've got some,
 So bring some out here.

We Wish You a Merry Christmas

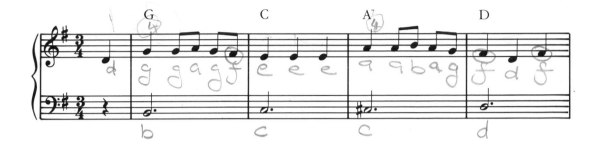

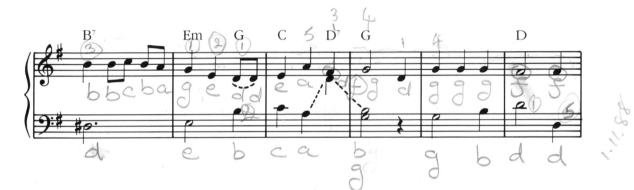

Index of first lines

The Publishers thank the following
for providing the photographs in this book:

Ardea/Richard Vaughan 9 above; Bridgeman Art Library 52, 58;
Mary Evans Picture Library 40; Spectrum Colour Library 13, 48;
TV Times/Transworld Features 5, 28;
Woodmansterne 9 below, 10, 44;
Zefa 6-7, 8, 36, 58.

Illustrations by Helen Stringer